Introduction

An adventure that begins with taking the initiative to change and do better. To break routines and go in search of a dream. Personal and professional fulfillment in a new universe full of unknowns.

Many wonder what exists in the virtual world that is so real that it entails whoever enters there?

Well, the universe of virtual currencies is just that, a new world completely innovative with the dogmas and the vicissitudes of

everyday life, which fills the unknown of each one.
A little strange to get into but easy to not let go.

We were taught as kids to live in a stereotyped daily life where history is pre-written and it is up to each one to give their brushstrokes. Leaving for work early to arrive as soon as possible, spending time with the family that we would have to raise early. We were not going to be too old for that. A salary, a security to face expenses, dreams always restrained and that fit in the palm of the hand so that we would always focus on work, not neglecting the dream but, always on a basis of utopia and distance similar to that of the earth the moon. It is possible to go there, but it is easier to observe it.

This was taught us, not to lose the real and the safe, to give up the utopian and illusory.

The world of cryptocurrencies is much more than a stranger's dream. It is the accomplishment of each one of us to trace his path and choose the path.

In this book my aim is to get to know a little more about him, to be aware of all possibilities but fundamentally to have knowledge of a very real universe that forces tend to hide, if it were not to avoid good profits from those at the top of the pyramid of power. Congratulations on taking the first step towards different knowledge of the reality and history you can write, the power to decide what you have.

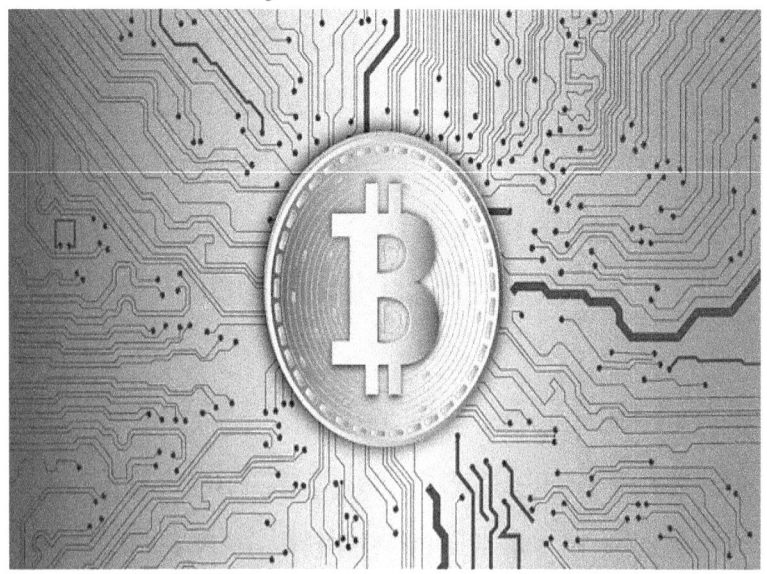

1 Historical contextualization

Before understanding what is virtual money it is important to make a connection with physical money.
At its origin came the need to develop a system that would allow the exchange of goods and services as well as an easy way to generate prosperity and demand.

The value of money, as we know, is not only related to its production, but to what it represents. In order to be viable, it must earn the trust of the community where it operates, with an effective balance between what people can do with it and win.

There must be tacit recognition between its value and its use, which is most often related to a ballast that should be scarce like gold. Thus, backed by currency, the currency is less susceptible to inflation, its importance was always related to its demand, the law of supply and demand.

The dollar today is not convertible or not backed. Its ballast lasted from 1044 to 1971 when President Nixon canceled his conversion leaving the currency without any ballast. Nixon felt that the currency's value should derive from the trust it generates. There are several thinkers who defend a return to the then Bretton Woods model, asserting that gold has been claiming a place at the center of the financial system, opinions leveraged by the fact that large banks are once again buying large purchases of this metal.

In the opinion of several other thinkers, Nixon's stance was largely the source of global crisis patterns as it enabled governments to spend more than previously possible

Well, let's get back to the central issue, real money can be seen as a simple paper called a check or an ATM card, credit….

There are several reports and facts that prove that even before 1900 there were virtual currencies. Several companies used vouchers or stamps that could be exchanged for products or services. American Airlines itself in 1981 the first air travel mileage program. Today it is common for most companies to use similar systems that represent a virtual service payment or purchase system. In the last few years, several million euros were billed with the sale of this "virtual currency"

Another form of virtual currency has recently grown in Africa with the use of mobile equipment and the difficulty of opening bank accounts. Users exchanged prepaid conversation minutes for products or services. This deal resulted in trillions of dollars in transactions.

That is, when you start the discussion that virtual currency is not real or useless in the real world, have you ever stopped to think how wrong it is? Vouchers or the like have been used in various forms for the purchase of products and services, which we can call virtual currency. As long as everyone agrees on the value attached to the good, it can become currency.

The first big difference in a virtual currency is that it is not issued by any government. It can be issued by any entity in which a set of users agree on its value and transactions.

Virtual currencies do not need to have a real value, but a value that the community accepts.

2 The origin of virtual currency

Bitcoin considered by many to be the first virtual currency emerged long after what was actually the first virtual currency in the case backed by real gold, the E-Gold created in 1996. A peculiarity in which many fiat currencies do not count. In 2008 E-Gold had more than 5 million accounts. Security problems ended this project in 2009 and others that have emerged

3 Mining and the points that came to fill the virtual currency

To mine, that is, to generate, or to validate bitcoin transactions, a computer is required that has a specific program connected in network to a set of other computers of different owners. This computer system generates the values in a user's account from limits updated by the network itself. The network is decentralized point-to-point, which ensures that there is no central or issuing or listing entity.

In these intervals that the system controls, a hash is issued that contains a certain encrypted value. Hash is the code that validates the transaction or allows you to verify the transaction. They are searchable and serve for the member to prove that it was valid and fulfilled.

One of the problems related to mining is the cost it causes to the miner, namely electricity.

There are several easy-to-search platforms on the internet that indicate the number of currencies possible to mine with a given machine as well as many other sites and forums where the average user can have information about which equipment to buy and how to configure it so that he "starts to make money"

Here is born another myth or natural skepticism from those who hear these terms and are surprised by the way they are transmitted. At first impression, it is immediately associated with something illegal or impossible, because we were all accustomed to the premise that making money will only be possible for a regulatory entity and all economic rules would jeopardize any other possibility unless it was illegal and falsification.

Come on then: far from being illegal, any user can do it, mine coins.

As mentioned, the miner receives a reward for his work. And anyone can do it as long as they buy the right equipment and configure it correctly.

As the blocks are checked, the miner receives his reward. And notice: there is no entity that gains from our activity and gives us a small percentage or that determines our volumes or gains. Everything is in our hands and with the same equipment that we mine today a certain currency, tomorrow we can change and do it with another one. Just change the settings.

The reader immediately asks, used to a centralized policy and which controls all activity for the "good" of the community, how long can this last?

There are several stories in this short period of blocking attempts. And there are countless failures in this attempt, the industry we know moves with large amounts of money
often ours, to end all competition, but it is a decentralized market.

What they do? Without mentioning names, movements of large companies / entities are known that create other parallel companies based in tax havens to make cryptocurrency purchases.

The maxim of; " if you can't with them, join "is applied. These movements are often accompanied by backstage moves that have been investigated and some of them proved.

One of the cases is related to a large company that for obvious reasons I will not mention his name but, I invite you to research, in which its CEO came to the public to consider that the future of bitcoin was compromised because it was a bubble and therefore investor capital would be at serious risk.

Hours later Bitcoin crashed, fear in the little ones took over and, coincidentally, in that moment of failure a company that proved to have links with that international fund, made brutal purchases of Bitcoin.

The market is full of tricks and here one of them is to maintain tranquility and conviction and not to be scared by the whales.

This is a term widely used in the market and it relates to the movements made by those who have more than 1000 bitcoins in this case on the BTC blockchain. These whales, without proof yet, often in a repaired way, try to mess with the market.

Imagine that your friend has about 10,000 bitcoins and you have another 10,000. And in the community where you relate there are so many others. A small "family reunion" and together they decide to sell the cryptocurrency 5% below the price in large quantities on some reference exchanges. What will it cause? Fear in the market and consequently sale.

For a moment the market goes into a spiral and, "the family" decides to buy again when it reaches the 10% drop. Not very profitable business? Right after a set of big sales comes a big purchase which leads to a quick recovery and increase in the value and number of units to these whales.

Anyone who has been in the market for some time is no longer frightened and can quickly and simply ignore movements such as these that can be identified, although these "families" present in all the global economic activity and that often come together, always create new ones ways to do it.

Great advantage of the crypto market: there is no member that controls them or a large entity, but all of us. There is no policy that directs it according to its interests, which is why it often revolts with this deregulated market.

3.1 Mining costs

Recent studies prove that the fear spread by environmentalists or, political forces or, economic powers, regarding the expenditure of energy to produce new monetary units are wrong and do not reflect the whole truth.

Compared to the cost of maintaining the traditional banking system today, mining is at much lower levels

Several entities, some with the intention of appearing and making their voices heard, often unknown to the public, others moved by unclear powers and, many others, by weak investigations, consider Bitcoin a Chernobyl a smoking giant in this regard. respect.

The question that these "thinkers" should also ask is what is the cost of maintaining the current banking system, what is the consumption of the servers with all these terawatts and branches or ATMs?

The consumption data originated by the BTC network are derived from Cambridge Bitcoin Electricity Consumption Indez Others as a source taken from digiconomist.net. However, the annual figures for this hourly consumption are totally divergent.

In the case of digiconomist.net the network captures 77.78 TWh while CBECI indicates 111.08 Twh. A small difference of 44% that normally affects these thinkers who attack this technology and ends their arguments. Although they remain for some time with support based on other interests. Thus, the thesis that the electric consumption of BTC is far from being a waste.

In the case of CBECI, informed sources indicate that the map is not even up to date and possibly would be in 2021.

In these reports, it is indicated that China captures 65% of mining consumption, which can obviously be totally wrong. Bitooda considered that China's power in this mining matter fell below 50%

Still on the subject of energy and environmental impact, 75% of mining companies use renewable energy sources, hydroelectric, wind, solar and geothermal. Several reports confirm this data.

Deutsche Bank Research National Energy Agency of China, Morgan Stanley and Coinshares point out that 78% of Bitcoin's electricity use comes from renewable sources.

Here, too, the blockchain network and its miners are ahead of the conventional market. Satoshi, is smiling because the miners are opting for green energy.

In the cost of the system, bitcoin critics do not consider all costs adjacent to the traditional banking system that uses far more than 140 Twh per year

Katrina Kelly-Pitou, who studies clean energy technology, considers that bitcoin's energy consumption is far from being as bad as they want to make it seem. It is then evident that the mining industry is not as wasteful as the current banking system, filled with servers, ATMs and agencies, but it is also free from fraud and manipulation.

4 What is blockchain

In a very simplified form the blockchain is an accounting book that records a transaction of virtual currencies, allowing it to be reliable and unalterable.

In other words, the blockchain records information on the amount of bitcoins or other currencies traded, who was the issuer (encrypted issuing wallet) and which the receiving wallet is. It also allows you to know when it was made and to which block it was associated.

In this way, transparency is total, this being one of the biggest attributes of the blockchain. It is not possible after a transfer cancels or even knows the senders or receivers.

All data is stored in groups of transactions and all blocks are marked with the record of time and date when they were carried out. In a short period of time, a new block of transactions is formed which is linked to the previous block, preventing it from being redone and changed. It would be necessary to change all the previous blocks.

4.1 Blockchain security

The blocks are dependent on each other which forms the creation and transaction chain hence the name of the blockchain

This technology is perfect because, as mentioned, it does not allow any kind of alteration or human management, so interference that may be placed is impossible. The registration of information needs this trust as for bitcoin transactions or any other blockchain network. As mentioned, each cryptocurrency has its own blockchain network. Within a blockchain network it is possible to create contracts or tokens.

The network is formed by miners who verify and record these transactions, as mentioned above, any node can be a miner provided that with the right equipment and, after analyzing the costs / profits.

For this mining work, miners put their computing power at the service of the network
As an incentive for this work to make the network safe and reliable, they receive a reward in the mined currency they can transact.

The miner can only add a transaction to the block if at least 51% of the network agrees with that transaction being legitimate and correct. All of these rules are in algorithm and are immediately checked by the machines and impossible to change. The consensus of the network is measured by this computational power.

Two chains of blocks can be formed simultaneously and the network will choose the chain that has the most work.

The aim is not to bore too much with technicality but to allow a quick understanding of this wonderful world.

So, in summary, the blockchain is this public book that records all virtual currency transactions in a chain of blocks in which everyone can participate as buyers, sellers or even miners

All of these transactions are reliable, unalterable and transparent.

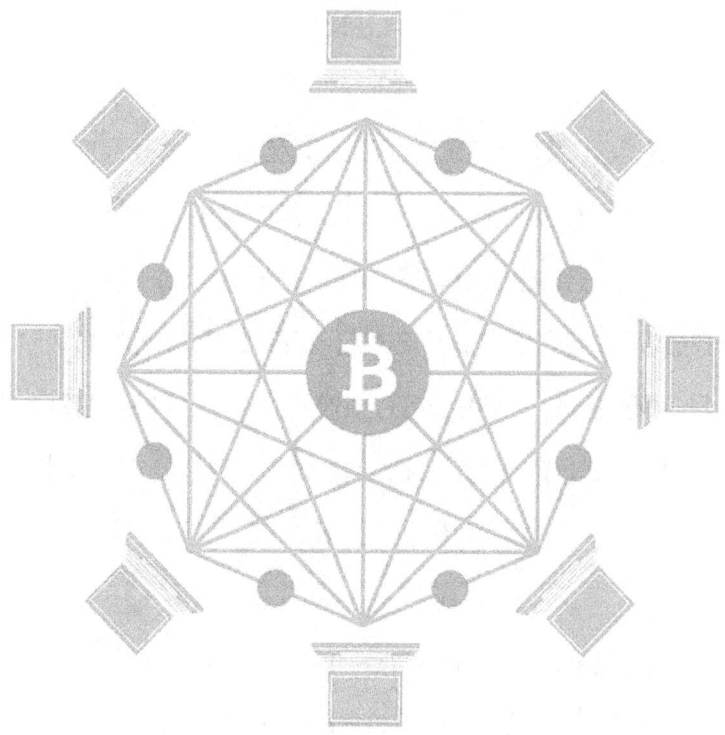

4.2 Blockchain in the real world

Bitcoin and cryptocurrencies were in fact the first applications to use blockchain but they are not the only ones

This technology is revolutionizing the world and all developed industries that are looking for speed, security and transparency. There are several innovations that have been achieved with the block network.

They are fundamentally innovative applications that bring new standards in the community, so it will be interesting to check their development and which ones will be confirmed in the medium, long term.

Spotify acquired the blockchain mediachain Labs in order to help develop solutions through a decentralized database in order to connect artists and licensing agreements.

Other ticket issuing companies use the blockchain network to prevent fraud and sale on the black ticket market.

In an industry harvested by pandemics and fears of spreading this complex network of owners and the retail industry, makes disease tracking more transparent and efficient in discovering which products may be contaminated in the distribution chain

Counterfeiting is an undeniable reality and with enormous costs in its fight, in addition to losses for brands. With the aim of introducing transparency, it is possible through blockchain to find solutions to combat counterfeiting, checking if they have been adulterated or diverted as well as stolen goods or fraudulent transactions.

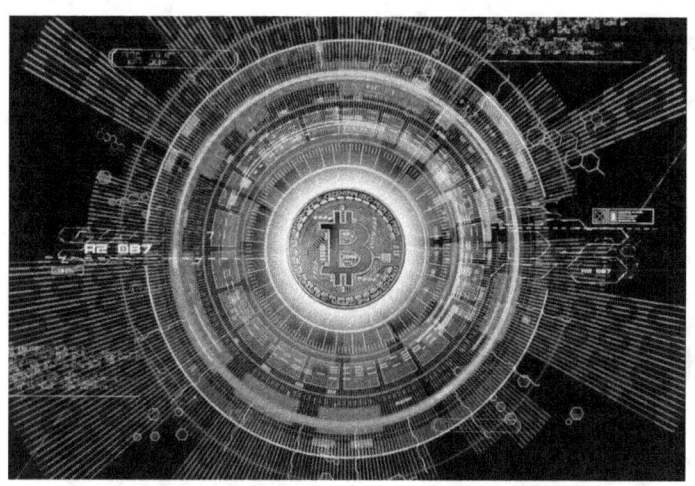

5 What is a cryptocurrency and how to use it in the real world

After all the introduction to this topic and the various items covered, it is useful to clarify what a cryptocurrency is really. Something that doesn't exist?

A few years ago when talking about a cryptocurrency, friends said that it was not real money and that "they didn't want to play"

It was always possible to convert these assets into fiat money, but the process was often complex and time consuming.

These days, they are immediate transactions that allow you to convert to local currency in seconds. Either through conventional ATM cards, or even by sending it to the bank account.

Imagine that you have a certain amount in bitcoins or another currency allowed for this type of transaction in a wallet. Simply convert the balance into local currency, and withdraw from any ATM or purchase at any store. In some cases the process is even simpler, and the conversion from cryptocurrency to FIAT currency is immediate and does not need a human hand.

As simple as having an account on one of the platforms you have the possibility to have an ATM card like Coinbase, Wirex and others and request a card. With it, just go to a cash machine and make withdrawals or use in a store for purchases respecting the daily limits that depend on the platform.

Another possibility, as mentioned, is to send to a bank account which takes an average of up to 48 hours.

You know then that a cryptocurrency is real, being different from the real one because it exists on the internet and cannot be touched, you cannot pick them up with your hands or keep them in your wallet or inside your mattress as they used to.

The term decentralized appears because there is no agency or government that controls or intermediates them, nor does it authorize the issuance of more currencies or validate operations. We do it, users.

The crypto are then created within a blockchain network through the mining process and circulate within a blockchain network that allows sending and receiving

They are generated online with linked information such as blocks that interconnect and create the chain, hence the name blockchain network and blocks.

All of this is done in encrypted systems, which allows this security and enables the issuance and transaction of virtual currencies in a secure manner.

This, by the way, is one of the great assets of cryptocurrency, the fact that it is encrypted, that is, it has security that is impossible to decrypt and extremely difficult to be fraudulent.

Can the reader question at this point what this cryptography is all about? Why does it make fraud and adulteration so difficult?

In a very simple way it is the way to confuse the information and shuffle being that only those who have the code can decipher it, in this case the blockchain network.

How can they be stolen?

Through common methods in the financial and social world.

In 2019, one of the largest exchanges in the world was hacked through phishing and viruses that attacked the platform. It was not the hacked blockchain network, but the platform that was responsible for all losses and compensated all those affected, continuing to work and reinforcing even its dominant position.

5.1 The differences between cryptocurrencies

The differences between cryptocurrencies are clear and should be made explicit in the white papers of each one. Give attention to a careful reading of this point.

Nowadays there are several technologies used to create a

cryptocurrency and its blockchain. It would be impossible to accurately mention all of them here.

I will move on to the main and their technologies.
Right from the start it is important that you understand the difference between crypto and token. At this point, it does not mean that a token has a value less than a crypto.

The token is preeminent and works within a blockchain network of a particular cryptocurrency. We give the example of the Ethereum network which is currently the largest public blockchain in operation, even bigger than that of bitcoin. Later on we will need some cases of contracts created within the networks

A blockchain network allows tokens and smart contracts to be created within it. Thus, it is quite easy to create a token at a very low cost.

If you have a project that you think is essential to create a cryptocurrency, forget the idea that the process is too complex and difficult. In fact, we can all do it.

What will differentiate them is their creator, the project behind it and its reliability for the market to accept it.

Thus, the reader before buying a cryptocurrency should be aware of several factors that I will explain later.

We give as an example the case of Ethereum within its blockchain. Later on, thousands of coins were created which, in order to be sent or received, need to pay a fee called GAS which is in eth. This need for eth made the currency more and more necessary and increased its demand.

There are tokens from many other currencies like EOS, TRON, DASH, LITECOIN…

Nowadays, the rates practiced and that can be verified before the transaction is carried out are extremely high for the ethereum network which will divert attention to other networks in a short period of time.

5.2 Cryptocurrency eco-systems

When it comes to the cryptocurrency eco system, it basically refers to the financial system that was created so that the currency really has value and utility.

A whole range of situations must be taken into account so that their value increases, creating added value for the investor. There are currencies that have been created and their future is exclusively confined to exchange and their transactions limiting their use in the real world.

A complete system should allow this currency, in addition to being tradable on exchanges, to be used on ATM cards, sent to the bank or accepted as an exchange on transactions.
This acceptance process has to be taken by its creators and accepted in the conventional market

Over time, there has been some fraud with these systems, with the creation of apparently perfect systems that later turn out to be fraudulent causing damage to its investors.

One of the main projects allowed the sale of millions of coins and was accepted in the market, creating a complete ecosystem. However, it was not possible to trade in the financial markets, which meant that its value was zero.

The ecosystem must take into account its veracity and its application in the social environment.

The analysis of an ecosystem must have several items to be evaluated, such as the history of its creators and dynamizers, the platforms where they are inserted, the novelty it brings to the market and its applicability.

As in the conventional market, the prospect of easy earning attracts vultures who, taking advantage of the natural ambition of the human being, obtain gains.

6 What is the difference between a cryptocurrency and a token

Basically a cryptocurrency has its own blockchain with its miners and is not dependent on any external blockchain, as a token works within an existing blockchain being dependent on it.

In terms of cost the creation of a cryptocurrency always obeys the creation of a blockchain and the creation of the pool of miners for the validation of transactions and blocks.

In the case of a token, its creation is immediate and the desired number of tokens is promptly mined and defined in its creation.

The creator places the tokens in his wallet and follows the instructions in the whitepaper.

I stress once again the importance of carefully reading this special document in all currencies where the entire plan for growth and distribution of the currency is written.

To take into account the foundation of its creation, the system that accompanies it as well as the volume of coins released in each period. As in the market economy, the greater the volume, the greater the supply, so the price will be lower and, consequently, the demand must accompany so that there is no settlement of the project.

In the case of a cryptocurrency, the control of the operation is not as centralized as in the case of a token in that part or all of the currency is mined and is in the hands of the market and the miners.

6.1 What is a token

One of the central questions surrounding this reality is whether the token can be considered a cryptocurrency. In reality, in the broad concept, no.

Although, on the circuit, they are all considered cryptocurrencies.

A token always circulates within a cryptocurrency blockchain.

In the case of Bitcoin, the first cryptocurrency, it works within its blockchain.

In the case of the aforementioned Ethereum project, in addition to its own currency, it has thousands of tokens issued within its network for transactions and storage.

Within these there are several varieties
I will mention two of them the utility tokens and the security tokens

In the case of utility tokens, they grant the right to use the platform and are equivalent to the network subscription.

Security tokens are based on values and securities like

cryptocurrencies and their value is always associated with supply and demand.

There are also fungible and non-fungible tokens, in the case of fungible ones all emitted in the network are the same. Even more clearly, as in the case of securities on the stock exchange, in which shares of companies are issued in equal parts, the tokens have the same value and size.

Non-fungible tokens are based on values united as works of art and widely used in games.
They guarantee the unique property of an asset that can be

virtual as in the game or representation in the real world

Tokens are public and immutable like those on the Ethereum network

The use of tokens has become massive within the cryptocurrency universe, given its ease of creation and implementation in addition to the low cost. Unlike cryptocurrencies that require electricity and mining costs for validations.

6.2 Bitcoin and its representation in the current panorama.

Bitcoin then appears as a breath of fresh air in the market, it is an undeniable reality and impossible to ignore for investors. There are several great figures who have been converted and who appear as important promoters.

During this period fashions have emerged within the novelty. Different approaches with profits for many and obviously losses for all who are unaware.

As with any novelty, immediate profit does not mean permanent. Past success is no guarantee of future success. It requires a permanent update and approach. Later on I will mention some interesting situations that are overcome and others that are expected to form.

The first big approach is for the niche that considers that

everything that goes out of government control is no longer worthwhile.

Like all those who consider that the only way to earn money is conventional work. Throughout history it has been verified that there is much beyond what we can see or even experience

The right decision will be up to those who decide to know

There are several clues that I gave in the course of this book and that some will be reinforced even as a first-person testimony in the final stage

This opportunity to enter a cryptographic world that is difficult to identify is evidently an interesting place where any parasite can lodge.

In any activity there are positive and negative points. The role of all newbies, where many will be experts, is to take into account the place where you move and the companies you want.

One of the points that I repeatedly emphasize is that the world is not for those who give up on the first setback.

When we learn to walk, we fall several times and never give up. It is in our nature, in our irrational side, to fight, to win and achieve.

Throughout our lives we are instilled in too many dogmas, too many limiting beliefs that often prevent us from showing our potential.

We have a duty to escape these traps in a slender way. Many take years to realize who is next, others take days and minutes. It will depend on our own personality and experiences.

In a bestial world like cryptocurrencies we know that it is extremely desirable and, where everyone wants a quick and brutal profit.

Without learning, common sense and thoughtfulness is not possible.

Study the history of operations well on the various sites.

Talk to the members involved.

See the history of the entity and its proponents.

Everyone has the right to make mistakes but repeatedly stops being a mistake to be an option for the easy and dishonest.

Watch for signs.

Read the trends and the paths that were followed by the project.

The history of the proponents is extremely important.
What they achieved outside of the presented project.
The experience of the team that takes the project.

Whoever drives a Formula 1 had to go through the different

categories. You will not be able to do it successfully if you are inexperienced.

What brings the project back to others and how similar ones managed to do it.

If you want to make a profession with cryptocurrencies, take courses that exist for this purpose, which will help you to be like fish in the water.

This is not a market for emotions, it is necessary to be cold-blooded so as not to falter at crucial moments.

The market is not the same all the time, it oscillates more sharply than any other, so the speed of decision and reading are as emotional as they are profitable or dangerous.

This approach that Bitcoin brings to the landscape was to build a fantastic progression reality for all winners, all who believe in its capacity and form of permanent evolution and overcoming.

Always think that the reality of the world goes far beyond what you see from our window.

With this statement from Bitcoin, many other opportunities have emerged that are sometimes even more profitable. We will talk about some later.

6.3 How to create a Wallet

There are several platforms that allow you to easily create a Wallet in order to save your crypto or token. For the start I suggest the Trust Wallet. Very easy to set up

All cryptocurrency wallets are encrypted so they are impossible to identify. It is common for your address to be periodically changed, which does not mean that you lose if you send it to your previous address because all the generated data are associated with your user. Reviewing the concept, when you send a cryptography it has an associated transaction hash. With this bash it is possible to confirm or verify the status of the transaction. Since it will only reach its destination after the number of confirmations that the miners validate. There are currencies that only need 3 validations and more. The reception process is completed when they reach the required number and the time can be seconds as few minutes depending on the volume transacted on the network.

7 Altcoin

What does this strange term mean among many others that appear on the market?

They are alternative digital currencies that currently make up more than 10,000. This number is scary for such a recent universe and can cause some fear given the difficult analysis of them and the approach on which to buy, on which to trust.

In fact, all altcoins should be created with the aim of offering solutions to the real world, bringing new paradigms and approaches.

The base was launched with blockchain and bitcoin and was exponential with other networks like ethereum itself.

Thus, all projects other than Bitcoin are considered altcoins. They differ in technology, approach, blockchain….

As mentioned in the previous point, all should present something new for the world financial and economic system, however, this is not true.

Some are only for financial speculation and, worse, scams to raise funds

Virtually all the projects presented have in common to add something compared to the mother currency, with greater speed, security and use.

It is always easier to project a new idea by comparing it to a success story and trying to show stronger points than not having any point of comparison.

There are some natural technical limitations of bitcoin technology such as scalability and transaction speed, which makes it today more and more valuable as an investment than as a means of transacting goods.

Altcoins use several resources that already exist in their

development base, but these alternative cryptocurrencies vary widely, different applications, algorithms used, greater digital security for users and many other features.

The use of altcoins has normal risks involved but I consider the positives to be much stronger and more pertinent.

I do not believe in a threat to the financial system although, many who are in that system fear it and, therefore, try to denigrate, block or speculate like bubbles or others.

It is an increment and a new approach to it.

We know that altcoins and Bitcoin will not by themselves solve all the problems in the world.

But the approach and the way it has progressed clearly shows an openness to change.

The system is tired of biased data, control of all operations and regulatory powers that move by hidden and evident interests.

The use of these assets reduces, for example, the costs of international transactions, bringing people even closer and strengthening the Global village that had its boom with the internet.

I venture to write that altcoins currently have the same impact that the internet had a few years ago.

The capture of investments is more democratized and free, for the creation of different and disruptive projects.

Altcoins' Market Cap shows us which are the strongest and which attract the most investors, which does not mean that it is in those that get the most profitability.

Bitcoin currently holds 65% of the market

Ethereum has the second largest market cap, followed by Ripple, Bittcoin Cash, Binance Coin, Chainlink, Cardano, Litecoin…

I would point out that this analysis of the volume of transactions does not define the relevance of the currency or even the possibility of success in acquiring it.

The future prospects and the market's expectations in relation to each one are extremely important.

There are some points that I reiterate must be taken into account

Promotion team qualification
Technology used
What brings new to the market
User Community
Purpose they propose
Popularity gained
Opinion of specialty websites

8 ICO contextualization

The first ICO was launched in 2013 for a cryptocurrency built on the Bitcoin blockchain in the case, Mastercoin raised $ 5 million. That same year, NXL obtained the equivalent of 6 thousand dollars.

Ethereum launched its ico in 2014 and wave in 2016

Ethereum raised $ 18 million and Wave $ 16 million.

This practice became fashionable and in 2016 several projects were financed through this model. Accounted for with amounts raised above $ 30,000, 64 were the ICOs out of a total of 103 million collected. In 2017, Boom took place at the launch of ICOs

In this period the fundamental thing was to separate the wheat from the chaff and fortunes were also made here and in other cases it was lost.

Projects based on sustainable, community-based growth have been hugely successful, as in the case of Ethereum.

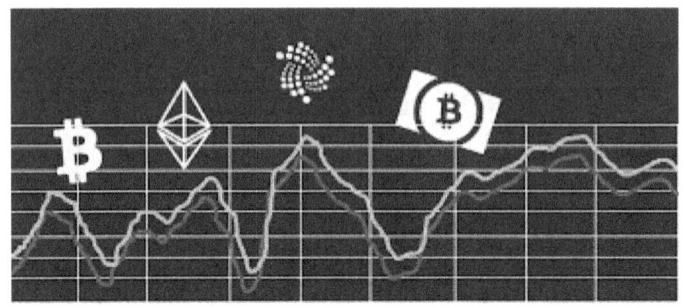

8.1 What does ICO mean?

The initial money supply is made with a phased launch of units on the market with different values according to their progression.

In each of the phases, the values are placed and those who buy in the first phase have an advantage because they acquire at a lower cost.

When launching a project, in order to capitalize, the promoters create launch phases at progressive costs.

With these funds, projects are leveraged and the roadmap phases are completed

A serious ICO that uses these funds in an anticipated manner will be able to achieve levels of excellence with some ease.

Here too, there have been several fraudulent attempts to raise funds and fail to comply with the established causing losses. As explained in the previous point, prior and careful analysis is essential to avoid the unwanted.

ICO is not regulated, funds are created for this new cryptocurrency project.

It was and still is, in a more lenient way, a way to boost startups and avoid bureaucracies or rigorous processes in raising capital that traditional investors were used to.

In the case of ICOs, they deal not only with investors but also with enthusiasts with an interest in investing in new projects and making profits.

Always taking into account, the whitepaper with the indication of all steps, objectives and a dynamic team. It should contain what the project is about, what it will fulfill after its completion, how much money will be needed for the steps presented and how long the ICO will be and its entry into the market

The acquisition of tokens does not make them partners in the company, but rather investors and owners of this asset, which must mention which exchange will be traded at the end of the Initial Currency Offering.

As a rule, ICOs are created within the ethereum blockchain network in the ERC20 standard

Any user can launch an ICO. For this you need the creation of the token, elaboration of whitepaper and develop a viable idea based on the blockchain network and the need for this token.

With the growth of this practice, the regulation tightened and hindered its process so that fraudulent situations were avoided so that before the creation of an ICO it is necessary to take into account all the legal aspects in each country.

Some jurisdictions consider the creation of ICOs like China or South Korea totally illegal. The USA with the SEC has prepared a detailed bulletin on this point alerting investors to the inherent risks.

Some ICOS may be considered by the SEC to be securities subject to federal securities regulations.

In Portugal there is a legal vacuum related to the subject of cryptocurrencies, so ICOs are allowed in exceptional cases as long as they are not considered fundraising, which is only allowed by entities credited by Banco de Portugal.

9 Airdrop what does it mean

This is a path followed by many entities for rapid growth and dissemination. In terms of marketing it works since the cost of advertising is low and the reach is high.

Airdrop, occurs at the beginning of the project creating a large number of users and curiosity on the part of the owners
That is, the average user gets free coins.

There are now several groups of coin hunters who simply look for AirDrops, meet certain requirements that are now imposed to earn them and then sell them.

Of course, limiting activity within this world to this procedure is absolutely reductive.

There are several reasons and motivations for communities to start these AirDrops, or donations. This is a good option for creating decentralization and broad distribution of assets.

As a rule, projects distribute around 5% to 10% of their offer. In recent times the value has been lower.

There are several examples that use this method to increase the number of HODL decentralization services (people who have coins at the expense of selling it)

With this increase the user will look for more information and the probability to buy in greater numbers is significantly greater.

There is a large number of users who receive AirDrops and later buy in the ICO processes mentioned above. Subsequently they reinforce positions in exchange and some become great owners

With airdop the search for information allows you to remain in the dispersed community

As a rule, airdrops are used to receive leads and thus enrich databases of those interested in this type of activity.

Between 2017 in the ICO boom, many projects started with AirDrops, most of which never got off the ground. With this method the user himself has a loving awareness of the asset and his interest in reinforcing position or ignoring it.

There are numerous platforms on how to find airdops that we highlight www.crypto-follow.com or Crypto Airdrops and www.airdropalert.com

How to analyze the potential of airdrop and project implementation?

It is important to analyze carefully some points such as:

-the ones listed on https://github.com with pertinent information
- careful reading of the whitepaper
- project website
-community that will propel you dynamizers and their history
-newness in the market.
-Do not forget to see social networks, especially the most targeted ones like Reddit or medium

How to get your airdrop?

Earning coins from airdrops follows different processes to obtain them.

To claim them you may have to:

put your email and belong to the group Telegram
like pages or share
Refer friends
Watch videos
Answer questionnaires about the project
Complete other tasks within the social network.

10 Cryptocurrency Exchanges, contextualization

Within a deregulated market, with its own capital, security is always questioned. Where can you safely buy and sell these assets without street intermediaries?

In March 2010, shortly after the creation of Bitcoin, the first cryptocurrency broker, aka exchange, emerged.

So far, the only way to do that was within forums or even chats.

The bitcoinmarket platform, meanwhile extinct, was suggested in the bitcointalk forum where several initial ideas about the cryptocurrency were launched. "Dwdollar" makes the initial proposal on January 15th, 2010.

He wrote: "" Hello, everybody. I am in the process of building an exchange, "he wrote. "I have big plans for her, but I still have a lot of work to do. It will be a real market where people can buy and sell Bitcoins among themselves."

"I am trying to create a market where Bitcoins are treated as a commodity. People will be able to exchange Bitcoins for dollars and speculate on the value. In theory, this will establish a real-time exchange rate so that we all have an idea of the current value of a Bitcoin, compared to a dollar."

The controversy over the value of bitcoin was very high and until the summer of 2010 the value was around $ 0.05. Bitcoin was priced at bitcoinnmarket at $ 0.003. That is 333 BTC per dollar.

Several bugs were detected in this initial process and corrected later with user feedback on the forum.

Paypal was often used to exchange and purchase the active crypto.

On June 4, 2011 Paypal stops operating due to several fraudulent transactions

Days later BTC were selling for $20

Bitcoinmarket was nearing its end, McCaleb programmer MT Gox launched in 2011, in 2014 it handled 70% of all global BTC trades.

Magicaltux (Mark Karpeles) buys the platforms and McCaleb focuses on the Ripple project.

In 2014, there was a major hacker attack that completely erased another memory that occurred in 2011. A small amount was stolen and all were refunded.

The first attack on a brokerage house in 2011 on 19 June led to the dollar being one cent. Hackers bought btc with their own accounts and took the earnings from the platform.

One of the users wrote his story like this:

"I'm Kevin and I'm the guy who bought 259,684 BTC for less than $ 3,000 yesterday. I really wanted to keep it a secret, but I can't. Here is my story about what happened ". He continued:
"I was watching, like many of you, a gigantic sales order burning the purchase orders. Mt. Gox doesn't execute operations very quickly, so we were watching this huge order slowly devour all orders to buy the books. The price started at around $ 17.50 and, in minutes, was below $ 10. At that point, I

realized that I was not just a big seller willing to accept some losses. It was someone trying to break the market by selling a huge percentage of the total Bitcoin in the market at once."

The value lost at the time corresponded to 2643 BTC in a total valued at $ 47,000. MT Gox fully refunded users

A second attack occurred shortly afterwards.

On June 20, 2011 Toasty was pondering what to do with Bitcoins, mybitcoin users reported that their accounts had been accessed and bitcoins were stolen.

It was evident that the MT Gox database had been replicated and names and passwords used in mybitcoin

June was a dark month for the market with the rise of bitcoin. Several small brokers were hacked and Mark Karpeles, owner of MT Gox covered the debts and migrated the injured to his platform.

Errors occur on the platform with its owner losing 2600 BTC when sending to an inaccessible address "s-272edf45031dd498e7b3ae89e11ff21b"

No one has ever been able to access that wallet, which proves that btc is safe and immutable

In February 2014 the platform went down. Mark Karpeles CEO of MT Gox left the board without giving details.

Shortly afterwards the statement came:

"Dear MtGox customers,
In view of the recent news and the potential repercussions on the operations of MtGox and the [BitCoins] market, we made the decision to close all transactions at the moment, in order to protect the service and our users. We will be monitoring the situation closely and reacting accordingly."

Seemingly real documents circulating on the internet indicate that 745,000 bitcoins have been out of circulation due to failures, creating a loss impossible to recover.

Coinbase, Bitstamp, BTC China, among others, issue a joint statement clarifying that the future of btc was not jeopardized, the market was reliable and the failures were caused by mismanagement by MT Gox

10.1 What is an exchange

Brokers facilitate the purchase, sale and exchange of digital currencies and tokens. The role is to connect buyers with sellers, enabling them to exchange quickly and safely.

Nothing prevents the user from making a direct p2p exchange, however, through a broker the data of who sells and who buys is not revealed. It is impossible to know the origin and the holder of the destination.

Copying the operating model of the traditional brokerage firms, fees were created for the intermediation and settlement service provided.

The first step to be able to work with the platform is the registration and in almost all cases, which we advise, mandatory Kyc verification

Orders are organized in a public book, whether for sale or purchase. The user must enter in the system the quantity and the unit value for which he wishes to buy or sell. Market values are dictated by the law of supply and demand. The exchange has no interference in this process. Wallets are available for users of accepted cryptocurrencies.

Cryptocurrency owners submit the request to the exchange for the listing of their crypto, and after analyzing the required requirements it can be listed

The sources of exchange revenue in addition to fees, are the value of the listing, advertising, promotional materials

11 Cryptocurrency trading

Nowadays the name of Trader is more and more in vogue. In fact, buying and selling crypto assets within a platform can, in itself, be considered trading.

It means assuming a cryptocurrency position against another FIAT currency.

Before starting this activity, whether with the intention of becoming professional or just obtaining extra income, get well informed about the assets you want to trade. When choosing a platform, you should take into account

- The number of currencies available
- Currency pairs
- The transaction volume in each pair
- The processing speed of the given order
- The history of the platform and its drivers

- The minimum values accepted to start
- The support given by it.

If you are used to conventional trading, not crypto, you will have to relearn how to work.

If on the one hand the graphics and technical analysis work very well, the oscillations are huge and very fast. Your attention will have to be doubled as well as the reading of various signals obtained in specialized platforms and international markets.

The recommendation is that through specialty websites such

as coinmarketcap, analyze volumes and projects well.

This website is not a European central bank. Many new users consider that the fact that the currency is listed on the platform is a sign that it is real and will be successful. Completely wrong. Coinmarketcap is linked by api to several other platforms from which it receives information and presents. It have news and indicators, but it is by no means regulatory, or synonymous with veracity.

Recently, the idea was created that for a currency to be real it would have to be accepted. First, there are several assumptions to appear there, I will not bore the reader by exposing all of them, but a recent currency will not be easy to present unless it reaches high immediate volumes in more than two exchanges.

In other words, if someone tells you that appearing in coinmarketcap is a sign of great success, get off.
And the opposite is also wrong. It does not mean that for not being is a fraud.

Returning to the subject of how to start this activity, get well informed about the assets

Learn to read graphs in a technical way and that way you will avoid some losses. These are not synonymous with the fact that the market will react in a certain way to something, but they are able to predict some situations. Numerous experts pointed out that by 2020 Bitcoin would reach $ 20,000, however, others pointed to $ 50,000 based on this reading. The cryptocurrency market is far more unpredictable than conventional ones.

However, they can be ways to avoid losses or even achieve gains. The traditional analysis used in stocks or currencies does not work in the world of crypto.
One more reminder:
if a conventional Trader tells you that he is starting in crypto but has years of success in the conventional stock market, be wary. It is not a guarantee of success.
Check carefully the fees charged for transactions. If you do not, you run the risk of forecasting a certain profit and in the end, it will be much lower or even zero. I will not, in this matter, suggest any specific exchange, just indicate

those that have the greatest volume

Binance
Coinbase
Cryptopia
Hitbtc
Bithumb
Okex

12 The trader

When we talk about the crypto trader we have to take into account your ability to read all factors. However, more than technical skills, it is essential that you have the mental and personality skills that allow you to act in a timely manner

The purpose of this book is not to make an analysis of the psychological or operational capabilities of the human being, however, in the course that I experienced, I have seen fantastic technicians with a brutal knowledge of the market having results well below expectations and others, with cold blood to have fantastic performances.

Human capacities for reading, analysis and time to act, beyond emotion, are crucial. The human being is naturally an emotional being, the Latins even more so.

The experience gained is also a very important factor. At the beginning of this activity, when the market drops 10%, the temptation is to stop Lost and limit the break. This is not always the way. It can be movements that intend this to happen. With experience it is also possible to detect these cases and not make mistakes.

I've experienced falls greater than 20% as well as climbs in one day.

Guaranteeing a monthly fee is a high risk, and once again all the points already mentioned must be taken into account.

12.1 The different trading models

Within trading there are several ways to trade and currency pairs to choose and work with.

There are traders who always make short-term trades with quick inflows and outflows and small profits or losses.

These operations are usually low risk and limit losses as well as gains.

A long-term operation without stop lost has a more risky nature but with a higher profit potential. At the time of purchase, Trade defines the sale price and subsequently a new entry in the pair or a change in the asset.

12.2 Types of trading

Day, (lasts less than 24 hours)

Being closed on the same day, it can take minutes or hours. It is the shortest in the types of trading and most used by professionals. Usually the purchase is made at the opening of the market and the sale is closer to the close. However, it can take seconds and small values.

It is very aggressive and quick to read and typical for those who have experience operating, often with the aid of a boot. It is common to obtain small amounts and close position. The work focuses on the sum of small operations. High volume currency pairs such as BTC / USDT are usually chosen

Swing
(two to five days)

It consists of a short-term operation but bigger than the previous one. On average it negotiates between 2 to 5 days. The objective is to remain in order until reaching the sale and exit. This method requires less parallel operations although it does not require permanent attention, a lot of patience and discipline and

time to follow graphs and trends.
A distraction can mean loss.

Position Trade
(a few weeks or months)

The aim is to achieve greater profitability compared to other types of tradind. There are usually few orders open at the same time. Liquidity is more important here than in the previous cases because the volume of purchases is higher to achieve profit. The sales term is longer and the ambition for higher percentages of profit is higher

Buy & Hold are long-term orders usually over 5 years. They are a kind of retirement savings plan. The investor buys and expects that in this period it will increase substantially.

Later on I will share some experiences

13 Arbitration

Given the large number of existing exchanges and the number of fans in this market, a very interesting practice has emerged with a very low error rate as long as the process is fast.

In the traditional financial market, the arbitrage process consists of looking for different prices for the same asset and buying at the lowest and selling at the highest.

In crypto the process is the same but with other factors involved. The difference in countries, rates, time zones, markets ...

Let's imagine that you register with 2 exchanges and put some assets for purchase as BTC

In exchange 1 ETH is 0.01 BTC and in exchange 2 it is 0.02 BTC. You will sell on exchange 2 and buy on exchange 1.

This process must be quick before the values are equivalent and the value of the fees must be considered. Today these differences are reduced, although they exist. It is necessary to have a good ability to distribute assets on these platforms, be aware and be quick.

One of the advantages of this type of operation is that it does not depend on the rise or fall of the crypto, in other operations analysis is necessary betting on its increase or decrease. Execution depends on analyzing differences.

One of the major disadvantages is that the action time will have to be extremely short.

What is true this second may not be the next. There are also bots that help in this process but…. We'll talk about bots in the next section

14 Bot

Many have heard of operational robots. Machines programmed to perform certain procedures automatically.

At the beginning of the bots, they held the assets in external accounts not controlled by the owners. Their lack of access and follow-up prevented them from withdrawing funds at any time.

Currently the new generation uses api and works directly on the customer's account.

The professional trader has some notes to make about this method:

"It is possible to create a winning trading bot, but it is not the robot that is magical. The winning factor is the strategy behind the robot, the creator of the bot needs to have a previously developed strategy, the point is this. Bots are nothing more than automating a strategy, so if there isn't something that works, the robot won't work. It is necessary to study, test, evaluate and only after that make the robot available. "

"First of all, for us," bots ", as they are widespread in the cryptocurrency industry - as a' magic tool 'that will provide excessively high and fixed profits - are pure illusion. We believe that bots are complementary tools for users who already do crypto trading, as long as they have good risk management. For example, allocating a larger portion of your Bitcoin portfolio to hold and a small percentage to automated

trading can be interesting. At the same time, depending on which tool you choose, you can even work with a kind of hedge in your portfolio, as is the case with our bot that works exclusively with Tether, the crypto-dollar (USDT). Finally, in our view, bots are an extremely efficient trading tool, since they are able to execute tasks at a stupidly greater speed, as well as, they are not subject to emotional factors and, for the most part, are easy to use by users. "
Crypto Universe

"Yes, it is possible to make a profit using a robot in operations. These chances become more real if you understand how the cryptocurrency market works, understand technical analysis and understand programming to the point of creating your own bot, so it would be stupid to share a strategy that is working. To be honest, I no longer believe in options for selling or renting these bots because the more people using the same strategy, the lower the chances of getting it right, even because of volume in operations. Trade with R $ 5,000, R $ 10,000, is one thing. Try trading with millions to see what happens. "

youtuber of the Epaminondas cryptosphere

In my analysis, a bot can be profitable, however, if traded en masse, it will repeat movements leading to losses. If thousands of people use the same bot your system will break down quickly.

The use of an api does not mean that the asset is safe. The owner of the bot can easily indicate the purchase of an asset and sell it by usurping the user.

In short, it is possible to use it as long as you are sure you have taken all the previous precautions, do not put your funds in the hands of messiahs or promises without previous results. Do not use bots sold massively.

15 DeFi the new opportunity.

As the market is constantly updating and evolving, a new approach is emerging every moment, if blockchain itself were not a source of possibilities to explore.

Experts point to the DEFI trend as the near future with several tokens achieving brutal valuation results.

First of all, decentralized finance.

They allow you to use cryptocurrencies in products like loans or insurance.

Some point out that the revolution could be bigger than bitcoin itself.

As mentioned, the name Defi means Descentralized Finance,

an English term for decentralized finance.

Financial services using crypto based on algorithms written primarily on the ethereum blockchain network

These schedules are introduced in the form of a smart contract on the network. They are automated and executed between the parties without the need for a human hand to intermediate or even institutions or bodies.

This protocol is much more complex than the transfer of values. These schedules determine rules and metrics that, when reached, trigger automatic execution.

These automatic agreements can serve several purposes, such as loans, currency conversations, insurance….

One of the main features is the elimination of intermediaries.

It is possible to pay off a loan using the pre-entered code.

A multitude of features previously only restricted to some players were thus open to cryptocurrencies.

Stablecoins became popular within DeFi, cryptocurrencies with value tied to a fiat currency without intervention and managers or companies.

One of the cases is the Wrapped Bitcoin that solves the problem of communication between networks. The value of WBTC is equal to that of BTC, it is attached to this.

In the traditional market, when a person asks for credit, they will obtain a fraction, given the value of the guarantee if they have it, and will pay a much higher percentage per year in DeFi, which charge about 1% per year and lend 100% of the value of the crypto given as a guarantee for any customer that activates this mechanism

This situation is made possible by the lack of intermediaries such as brokers, consultants, regulators and their costs.

Another of the situations that makes it feasible is the fact that DeFi transactions are with cryptocurrencies recorded on the blockchain since it serves as a guarantee, being blocked preventing the guarantee from being transacted

There is also the possibility of cryptography to be used in decentralized Exchanges, automatically exchanging one cryptography for another with a lower rate than that of a company.

One of the guarantees of the DeFi project and technology is that the contract is public and can be opened for analysis if you have the knowledge to do it

It is obviously a completely new world for anyone entering the cryptocurrency market.

Uniswap: is a decentralized exchange that has US $ 1.3 billion in cryptocurrencies blocked in guarantee. It also has a governance token, UNI

Chainlink: it is not exactly a financial product, but a kind of midfield between networks that do not speak the same language. It also connects smart contracts to the outside world, such as payment systems and databases.

Aave: like Compound, it is a low-rate loan DeFi that allows the lender to earn interest. Launched in July, it has $ 1.37 billion blocked in cryptocurrencies.

On the DeFi Pulse website you can see the most used projects. As it is a new concept, it is important to analyze whether the projects are actually decentralized, which project, the code and the team behind the project.

16. Whitepaper

On the 31st and October of 2008, the first cryptocurrency whitepaper was created, having been fired for several emails from those interested in cryptography.

Satoshi wrote in the mail: "I've been working on a new electronic money system that is completely point-to-point, without the need for trust in a third party",

Follows link that was sent with the document
https://bitcoin.org/bitcoin.pdf
A whitepaper It is a document that serves as a guide to explain a certain concept or the solution to a specific problem.

For analysis of a cryptocurrency project this document is crucial. It is there that all the bases and phases of the project must be described.

Given the increase in the number and cryptocurrencies, this

document is no longer taken into account, giving rise to a greater number of frauds.
This document must be clear and noticeable

- Problem that the project solves.
- How that solves it.
- Project capitalization (financing rounds, minimum capital, maximum capital, stages of development, etc.).
How tokens will be distributed and how they will be invested in development.
Team involved.
Roadmap or deadlines for development.

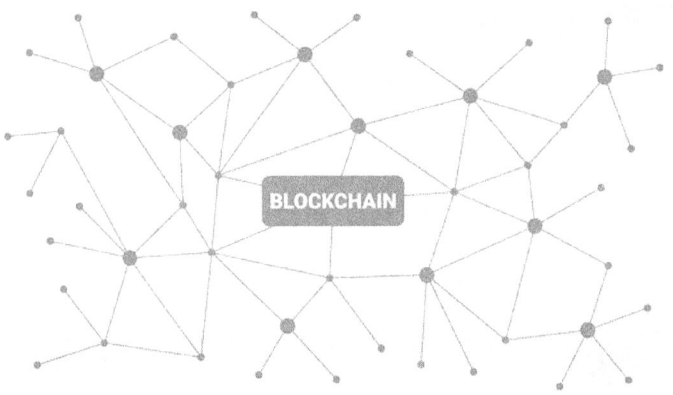

17 Present of crypto

Currently cryptocurrencies are being used not only as a source of investment for trading or even capitalizing on projects that they intend to innovate, but also as security in an unstable market.

Major global finance companies have made large investments that increase their market value
At the beginning of 2021 the market reached a capitalization of 1 trillion dollars.

According to Coingecko the market continues to grow
Bitcoin continues to dominate with over 65% of the market.
Only in January 2018 did this figure reach 800 million dollars. Large financial companies like JP Morgan and Bank of America or even Paypal are strong in this market.

According to analysts this is the perfect time to enter the market. A few years ago friends told me that buying $ 1000 was expensive, they should have bought $ 100

Not long ago with him for $ 10,000, I was told it was too expensive and they should have taken the opportunity to buy it for $ 1000.

And today? What will those who have not bought in the current situation will say in the near future?

18 The obstacles

One of the major obstacles to the growth of cryptocurrency is the fact that its value is still very fluctuating. As a means of exchange, medium-term security in transactions is not viable. A balance equivalent to $ 10,000 can days later be worth $ 7000 as $ 13000

Volatility has been maintained over time. According to analysts, the possibility of stabilization will be more advantageous than the hallucinating increases in value. Some variations in value are still inexplicable, which also makes it difficult for new players to enter.

Another obstacle is related to the large number of coins with fraudulent projects, which removes the credibility.

19 The future

The enthusiasm is growing and despite some criticisms by well-known economists that delay their assertion, the power games that surround them discredit them and strengthen the crypto market.

It is impossible to accurately predict the future or the value they will reach. However, it is undeniable that they are here to stay and assert themselves as a viable alternative. Capitalization is increasing which reinforces this belief.

Large entities are increasing interest and progressively investing in the market. With new projects emerging and new variants within blockchain networks that
features, as described, have been adopted for various situations and to solve several problems

"I don't like to foresee - even if it doesn't look like an investment indication - but everyone in the market knows that I'm very optimistic about Bitcoin. The price will remain volatile in the short term, but investors should continue to focus on the long-term result ".
BINANCE CEO Changpeng Zhao

"We will continue to experience economic turmoil. With that, it is clear that global individual and institutional customers will increasingly turn to the Bitcoin network. It is absolutely inevitable that digital currencies are increasingly accepted and spread".

Beibei Liu CEO Novadax

"The expectation is that new giants, as some billionaires and big companies did this year, should give in and announce that they are working with Bitcoin, or acquiring Bitcoin, further placing this asset as a store of value. This will definitely have an impact on the price, in the last halvings (when the offer is cut in half) always in the following year, Bitcoin had a historic price increase surpassing up to 10 times the previous tops ". Foxbit CEO Joao Canhada

"Amid an uncertain macroenvironment and similarities with the gold market of the 1970s, Bitcoin could reach more than US $ 318 thousand in 2021. Its assessment is made using technical analysis, following a similar trajectory of cryptocurrency in the last seven years. "You see the price action being much more symmetrical over the past seven years, forming what appears to be a very well-defined channel, giving us an upward movement in terms similar to the last high (in 2017)" Citibank Director Tom Fitzpatrick

"This is why many people have fled to Bitcoin […] because it is not clear how the dollar gets out of this debt and impression trail, and what it will really be worth in the future, if anything."

Tayler, one of the twins who won fortunes from Mark Zuckerberg after a legal battle and bet heavily on cryptocurrencies

The twins believe that Bitcoin will reach $ 500,000 in the next decade. "It is an emerging store of value and is better than gold," said Cameron. "We think we could value something around 25 to 40 times today's price". For Tyler, this projection is "really conservative".

20 Testimonial

Dear reader, after reading these points and knowing this world, I believe that your desire to start in a wonderful new world is tremendous.

I will share a little of my experience that I believe can help you not to make the same mistakes that I did as well as, to take more advantage of the knowledge acquired throughout this book.

As I wrote in the course of it, history is written on the go and in this journey a lot comes to us, it is up to each one of us to make the choices so that the path taken is the best one.

Impossible that it is only about victories and successes. The most brilliant men in history have gone through many troubles.

From Steve Jobs to Einstein among many others.
What made them really excellent was not only their comprehensive vision or capacity for innovation. Yes, it was his determination to impose his desire.

"The genius of physics and awarded a Nobel Prize, was categorized in childhood as" mentally slow ". He only managed to speak at the age of 4 and read at the age of 7. They thought it was hopeless and he was also refused admission to the Zurich Polytechnic. Before proving his theory, he was the target of teasing in the scientific world, because they said he was just a dreamer. Yeah ... but Einstein stayed in the story, because those who underestimated him, those are forgotten. "

"Steve Jobs went down in history as a successful man and someone who left us a series of inspiring phrases like:" You can view a mistake as a blunder to be forgotten, or as a result that points to a new direction "or" Have courage to follow what your heart and intuition say. They already know what you really want. Everything else is secondary. " However, his path has not always been brilliant. He dropped out of school and had to leave his own company, Apple. At 30 he was devastated. However, he considered this "fall" to be a positive thing. It was thanks to her that he changed his way of acting and entered one of the most creative periods of his life. He returned to Apple and, under his guidance, the company started to rise, having created several iconic products such as the iPod, iPhone and iPad. "

We as a Portuguese people have a history full of remarkable moments in which at a certain moment we were able to leave our mark. And, in my view, we all have a legacy to leave. Some more ambitious, others more restrained.

The starting point is; where do you want to get?

I was raised in a family with conservative principles imposed by my grandfather of rigor and discipline. But, always focused on success. I was soon told that the family foundation stone would have to be created, preserved and valued.

A good education would allow a good job and with it a good quality of life.

Well, being conformed is not in my DNA. It is difficult to accept a formed universe, life is what is imposed on us as correct.

It is not rebellion but a way of life that does not have to be by the book.

Here lies a point of difficulty for everyone who enters a different and constantly adapting world. In fact, it is not for everyone that is formatted. It is necessary to do a reset and permanent refresh or, the difficulty will be great.

After years of managing sales teams in the mainstream market, I heard Bitcoin.

Imagine someone looking for a destructive way to succeed and who wants to learn more.

I entered the world I met fantastic people, equally ambitious and others less good, normal.

I tried to separate the wheat from the chaff, and to accompany those who dominated the technical part of the process, to absorb as much information as possible so that I could use it. I read a lot and researched. Soon, as I always do,

I started to establish stages. Where I wanted to go. Making money is a buzzword that I personally don't like, it doesn't attract me.

I saw some having very interesting earnings already in 2015.

Here I established for myself that success or failure in this world would always be on my side. I did not grow up in an environment where blaming others was practiced. I have always been taught that I am responsible for my actions and my path. Nobody is to blame when I don't succeed or fail, just like the victory has a big slice of me.

There, I decided to go to the fight.

And in this way, often very difficult for an inexperienced person, it is important that you are attentive. Not only to the market, but also to business. Don't get carried away by brilliant projects without first investigating them thoroughly.

And understand that your analysis will always be conditioned by your willingness to move forward.

In other words, you are invited to a project and the illusion takes over you, you believe that it is what you are looking for. Your brain is intoxicated to head in.

But his rational side cuts the impulse and asks him to be sensible so he can look for more. And so it does, only… .. you are already conditioned by the previous premises of glory and success, in a fantastic way because you have a warrior and innovative spirit.

Many will not have this problem. Either because the fear is greater than the will, or because the rational side does not let the creative take control.

The old people of Restelo manage to move them with some ease and never try to face Adamastor.

Comfort is enough for the harvest of happiness. Going in search of the unknown is not part of those plans. But don't leave, because you can still enter the world of crypto and win.

After your analysis, conditioned or not, you decide to go ahead and reach the next step.

Here I always suggest that you do not look at the top but at the next meters. The road will be shorter, partial victories will be celebrated and their determination will be reinforced.

Imagine a football player. At the beginning of the season he has hundreds of training sessions ahead of him and more than 30 games to achieve his goal.
What you have to think about is to win in the next training session to be selected in the next game and in the end achieve glory

If the player thinks only about the last game, he will be too distant and will not get the necessary motivation to achieve what he proposes.

Your decision is made and you go ahead. So it has happened to me a few times. In some cases I quickly realized that the decision had been made badly and quickly changed the trajectory.

Because assuming an error in a decision is not a failure.

If you are wrong and you know it is, and yet you continue, then yes, you are failing.

There have been times on this journey when I have spent more time than I wanted to develop projects because there are situations where you cannot just turn your back and move on. You will create dreams, illusions, and do not give up on them while you have some chance of reaching them

Notice, very important:

We live in an era of globalization and some self-centeredness caused by all the social networks that isolate us from the reality of interpersonal contact.

Therefore, our ability to be grateful is reduced. To blame is greater. To magnify the ego is reinforced.

When you suggest a winning project to someone, don't expect recognition.

This will not normally happen. The human being will reap the rewards for his decision to have risked.

If your suggestion doesn't go well, expect to be blamed. After all, you were the one who suggested it.

That's how it works, not only in this world of Bitcoin, Ethereum and company.

For a time my determination was so great that it made my own reason intoxicating.

I lived the projects as part of me and was even able to guarantee that they would be successful.

This is a big mistake. Don't do that. Even if it seems to you to be 100% reliable and successful, warn that something can go wrong and that the onus is on the decision maker, as well as the gains or losses.

I was entering an aggressive, dynamic, fantastic world. My training, my experience seemed small for the giants I was meeting. Everything seemed so… brilliant. And it actually is.

But, I was at a high level.
The most capable dream sellers always move where there is gold. Because they are capable.

Feel who will transmit the message to you with the emotion of blindly believing, given your determination and reading, and who wants to suck your energy.

Avoid the traps that as described in some religions, the negative is demon or similar, it is beautiful and wonderful because it is the illusion in the strongest state.

Welcome to step number two.

One in which, after the illusion, he takes a bath in reality and realizes that not everything that glitters is gold and that, after all, he will not kick and discover a pot full of beautiful and shiny pieces.

For a moment I felt incapable and lost, after all I had abandoned my comfortable life for the purpose of succeeding in a fantastic universe.

For a moment my parents' voice sang in my brain.

And my legacy was more distant.

But, it was not in a bottomless pit. I never lost focus, sometimes I fell, cried and despaired.

Some of my life maxims are:

-Never give up
-Never blame.
-Never lower me

The path to success can be taken seriously. It is not necessary to be unable to cheat or cheat. If this happens during our journey, let it be inadvertently.

To make cheating a way of life is to reduce our essence to waste. It is living in depression and gloom. Be hated by yourself.

As my belief in a better tomorrow is infinite, as my determination is permanent and the maxims given are taken into account, I only had one way. Raise stronger and continue the fight.

The one that I will fight until the last day even if I win in all of them. There will always be one more goal to achieve. A stage to win.

I met brilliant minds, some lost and out of focus, others oriented. I absorbed more information, I gained experience for new flights.

I embraced projects, developed knowledge and innovations.

I had people with me who hugged me when I needed to.

I was fortunate to contribute to the evolution of many people. On a personal and professional level.

Life is not a one-way street. It only makes sense if you embrace causes, people, projects.

There are fantastic people lost, incredible projects abandoned.

Perhaps because they were not as lucky as I was, to be instilled in how brilliant a brain is.
The hunger for victory and healthy competitiveness

Help them to look at you and determine your path. It will make you feel more special.

Do not punish yourself too much for your failures. Learn from them. They are part of your evolution process.

In digital currencies, expect to experience the extreme in everything.

It will make you stronger and more resistant

If an ICO seems beastly and will change your life forever, look for all the information. Read the whitepaper carefully and see which platforms the token or crypto is listed on.

How much time you have and what you bring back. Not everything that shines is gold. I learned this almost literally.

Who the promoters are and what they have done throughout their lives. Look for specialty websites to learn about the surroundings.

If you want to buy a cryptoactive watch its development in the last few weeks.

If you want to trade, start with caution and precaution. Do not put all your eggs in one basket.
Do not invest more than 10% of your free assets.

Fundamentally, be happy.

Present receipt of buying this book and benefit from one of the courses at:
Write to
geral@academiadamente.pt and learn how to improve yourself with NLP or with a course

www.academiamente.pt

www.ingramcontent.com/pod-product-compliance
Lightning Source LLC
Chambersburg PA
CBHW052352220526
45465CB00003BA/1071